Praise for *Speaking Well*

"*Speaking Well* is a gem for both the experienced and novice speaker. Adam Hamilton offers straightforward, practical suggestions for better construction and delivery of high impact sermons and presentations. Full of well-tested reminders, it's a great resource!"

—*Heather Bradley and Miriam Grogan, Founders, The Flourishing Company, LLC*

"Adam Hamilton has emerged as one of the most influential preachers in North America. In this book he shares how he does what he does. Lively, smart, and right to the point, this book brims with practical wisdom."

—*Ted Smith, Associate Professor of Preaching and Ethics, Candler School of Theology, Emory University*

"When Adam Hamilton speaks, people listen. In *Speaking Well*, you'll discover why. This clear and immensely practical guide should be within arm's reach of every speaker—and especially every preacher. My sermon this weekend will be better because of it."

—*Roger Ross, Lead Pastor, First United Methodist Church, Springfield, IL, and author of* Meet the Goodpeople

"*Speaking Well* coalesces the crucial essentials for any speaker into a quick-read format that is nutrient-dense. I hope every seminary adds this as a required text, and I plan to utilize it for pastors and unpaid leaders in my own work with church revitalization. Well done!"

—*Sue Nilson Kibbey, Director of Missional Church Initiatives, United Methodist West Ohio Conference*

"*Speaking Well* condenses years of experience into a practical volume of quick and fun tips for improving any public speaker. If you have a message that you want to communicate effectively, you need to read this book."

—*Jacob Armstrong, Pastor, Providence Church, Mt. Juliet, TN*

"Adam has gifted us a delightful little book with big implications—becoming the most compelling presenter you can be! In it, he offers refreshing glimpses not only into his techniques and strategies but also into his heart: helping others for the sake of the kingdom!"

—*Jim Ozier, Director of New Church Development, North Texas Conference, The United Methodist Church*

"In this book Adam has given us a great gift. I just wish I had this book forty years ago. It will go on my recommended list for new pastors, and I hope seminaries will put it in the hands of all graduates."

—*J. Clif Christopher, CFRE, President of Horizons Stewardship*

Other Abingdon Press Books by Adam Hamilton

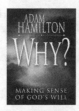

Why?

Forgiveness

*When Christians
Get It Wrong*

Half-Truths

ADAM HAMILTON

SPEAKING WELL

WELL

A Pocket Guide

ESSENTIAL SKILLS FOR SPEAKERS, LEADERS, AND PREACHERS

Abingdon Press™

Nashville

Library of Congress Cataloging-in-Publication Data

Hamilton, Adam, 1964-
  Speaking well : essential skills for speakers, leaders, and preachers / by Adam Hamilton. — First [edition].
     pages cm
  Includes bibliographical references.
  ISBN 978-1-5018-0993-4 (hardback)
1. Public speaking. 2. Preaching. 3. Oral communication—Religious aspects—Christianity. I. Title.
  PN4129.5.H36 2015
  808.5'1—dc23

                            2015028982

16 17 18 19 20 21 22 23 24—10 9 8 7 6 5 4 3 2
MANUFACTURED IN THE UNITED STATES OF AMERICA

*Dedicated to all who give themselves to
the task of public speaking, particularly
those who do so with fear and trembling
as they seek to speak on behalf of God.*

CONTENTS

Introduction — ix

INTRODUCTION

In the last thirty-five years I've delivered over five thousand sermons, speeches, lectures, workshops, keynotes, and eulogies. Malcolm Gladwell famously noted that it takes ten thousand hours of practice to achieve mastery in a subject. If you include the prep time, I'm way over ten thousand hours, but I wouldn't say I've mastered public speaking. I have learned some tips and practices that seem to increase the likelihood that the message will hit the mark. I doubt many of these ideas are original. We learn by our own experience and by observing others. In this brief book I'd like to share nineteen of these tips or practices with you.

A word up front to the preachers reading this book—this is not a book on preaching, but on speaking well. I promise every chapter in this book relates to your work, but I've intentionally written this book for a broader audience including business, educational, nonprofit, legal, and government leaders who are called upon to give speeches to groups of people. And to you who are not preachers, and perhaps not into religion at all, I believe you'll find that most of the skills and techniques required for effective preaching are important to public speaking in your line of work as well.

These are intended to be short chapters—the essentials. I picture this as a pocket guide to speaking well. In it I'll offer you nineteen short, simple tips to improve your public speaking. My hope is that you'll return to these chapters whenever you face a new speaking challenge or when you need to brush up your skills. OK, let's jump in . . .

ASK THREE QUESTIONS

We'll begin with what may be the most important component to giving an effective speech: asking the right questions. There are three very simple questions your talk, speech, or sermon should be built upon: why? who? and what?

WHY?

When I'm asked to give a speech, talk, or sermon outside of my home church, I want to know, **Why am I being asked to speak? Why me? Why are others being asked to listen to me?** The underlying question is really about the purpose, aim, or mission of the talk. Sometimes those who ask you to speak aren't clear about the answers to these questions. They may say, "Well, we needed someone to talk at our event and we heard you're a good speaker." Sometimes they follow this with, "You can talk on anything you want to, just be inspirational!"

Here's what I've found: The less clarity I have around the purpose, the mission, the goal, or the why of a talk I'm going to give, the harder it is to prepare and the less effective my talk is. The greater clarity I have around the mission or purpose of the talk, the more likely I am to feel the talk was effective.

When someone isn't clear about the why of the talk they hope I'll give, I'll spend time trying to help them work through this. I may begin by asking them to describe the mission of their organization and the purpose of the particular event where I'll be speaking.

For preachers preparing and delivering a weekly message for their local church, the sermon should serve the mission, vision, and goals of the local church. For those who speak in the workplace, it is critically important that your presentations and talks align with the mission and purpose of your organization. If you are in charge in your organization, and speaking, you must answer these essential questions for yourself—no one else will answer them for you.

WHO?

Once you are clear about the mission or purpose, of both the group you are speaking to and the particular speech you are going to give, your next step is to know to whom you will be speaking. What will be on their hearts and minds as you speak to them? What might they need to hear from you? I find this is an easier task with the congregation I serve, since I know them well. It requires more homework when I'm speaking to groups with which I'm less familiar.

I was recently asked to give a ten-minute talk to caregivers in the community—therapists, pastors, rabbis, and others who devote a great deal of their time to caring for people who struggle. I knew that the people in this audience often feel burned-out and overwhelmed from bearing the burdens of others. As I began to work on my talk, I thought about what I might share that would offer encouragement to this particular group and their unique situation. Know your audience, understand the challenges they face, and consider the questions and concerns they are wrestling with. This will enable you to offer a timely and relevant message.

When President Franklin Delano Roosevelt delivered his first inaugural address in 1933 the country was in the midst of the Great Depression. Fear had gripped the nation and hopelessness was in the air. What Roosevelt knew was that he needed to calm these fears, reassure the country, and communicate to the nation that "the only thing we have to fear is fear itself." Eighty years later, we still recall these words as some of the most compelling in any inaugural address, but they were written in response to FDR's clear understanding of people's needs.

WHAT?

Finally, in light of the why and the who, I begin looking for the what. I begin asking, "What do I want my hearers to know? What do I want them to feel or experience? And what do I want them to do in response to this message?" These questions correspond to the head, the heart, and the hands. You may recognize them as three of the four Hs of the 4-H clubs. The founders of 4-H believed that people learn and develop best when they engage their heads (intellect), hearts (emotions), and hands (action). This premise is important for speakers as well. Answer the what question, and you're more likely to include material that resonates with more people, on multiple levels, in multiple ways. You'll also be ready to begin writing your speech with a strong and focused idea of what your content should include.

As a speaker you should know why you are speaking, you should understand the people to whom you are speaking, and you should be clear about what you want those people to know, feel, and do as a response to your message.

THE FIRST TASK IN SPEAKING WELL IS TO ANSWER THESE QUESTIONS: WHY? WHO? AND WHAT?

Chapter Two
THINK LESS ME, MORE WE

Among the most often used words in our vocabulary are *I*, *Me*, and *My*. Effective speakers minimize the use of those self-oriented words in favor of *We*, *Us*, and *Our*.

If *I*, *Me*, and *My* dominate your speaking, you'll sound more self-absorbed than you actually are (or maybe your speaking betrays the fact that you *are* more self-absorbed than you realize). It is off-putting to many people. It also diminishes your audience, making them passive listeners instead of active participants. It is as if you're saying, "Just sit there and listen; this is all about me!"

I remember some years ago a national political leader who used *I* far more than he should have. Even his friends cringed at times, but most were unwilling to tell him. Those in his own political party often found his language irritating. For his political opponents, it was like hearing someone scratch their fingernails down a chalkboard. It gave people the impression that he was egotistical and that he didn't need or care about them. This is how our hearers react when we use *I*, *Me*, and *My* instead of *We*, *Us*, and *Our*.

There are times when you will need to use *I*, *Me*, and *My* language. It can't be avoided entirely, and there are times when telling your own story is important. The most effective use of first-person language is when you are sharing your own short-comings to illustrate a principle, or when you are poking fun at yourself. Though this can also be effective when emphasizing your own experience or convictions.

Excellent speakers try to avoid being the hero of their own stories. Again, at times you can't avoid it. The best illustration of a point may be a story that involved you and will be hard to tell without referring to yourself. But when possible, find a way to make a positive story about someone else, and leave yourself out. Sometimes, to set an example for the people in my congregation, I share a situation when I feel I did get something right. Instead of telling the story about myself, I'll say something like, "A guy I know . . ." and attribute the activity to this anonymous person. It is usually possible, and always preferable, to deliver a talk that focuses on others rather than our selves.

Minimize the *I*, *Me*, and *My*, and invite your hearers to be a part of your speech/sermon/talk by using *We*, *Us*, and *Our* language instead. Poke fun at yourself while ascribing the positive examples you set to an anonymous person you know. These are habits of effective speakers.

EFFECTIVE SPEAKERS USE *WE*, *US*, AND *OUR* MORE OFTEN THAN *I*, *ME*, AND *MY*.

Chapter Three
FIND THE RIGHT STARTING POINT

As we learned in chapter 1, most effective speakers have a goal in mind—something they want their hearers to understand or feel, some kind of action they hope their hearers will take, an idea they hope to convince listeners of. For the preacher it is usually a proposition from scripture—a truth to be believed, a hope to be trusted, and almost always a calling to be fulfilled. If you are a politician delivering a campaign speech, the ultimate goal is to persuade your hearers that you are the right woman or man for the job, though often politicians are speaking to the already-persuaded, in which case the aim is to raise money, recruit volunteers, or be overheard by the media. If you are in sales, you are selling a product. In most speeches or talks it's critical to have clarity around the goal of your talk.

Once you are clear about the aim of your talk, it is important to think about the structure of your message. The key question regarding structure is "where do I begin?" Do you start with the solution and then work your way to the problem? Or do you begin with the problem and then work your way to the solution?

In seminary most preachers are taught to start with the solution—typically found in a passage of scripture. They are taught that an effective preacher starts by exegeting the text (carefully understanding and explaining the meaning of the text to its author and original hearers). Next the preacher seeks to show which question, problem, or situation in contemporary life the biblical text provides the solution or answer to. Finally the preacher illustrates the way the scripture applies to our daily lives with a story that drives the point home. The structure looks something like this:

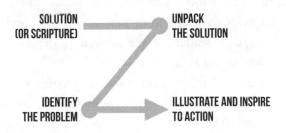

SOLUTION (OR SCRIPTURE)

UNPACK THE SOLUTION

IDENTIFY THE PROBLEM

ILLUSTRATE AND INSPIRE TO ACTION

Many mainline preachers turn to the Revised Common Lectionary, a preassigned set of scriptures for each Sunday of the year. The Lectionary offers four scriptures each weekend—a text from the Old Testament, another from the Psalms, a passage from the Gospels, and a selection from the rest of the New Testament. The assumption beneath this method of preaching is that regardless of what is happening in the world, or in the lives of the members of the congregation, one of these four texts will offer up an answer to life's problems, a timely word to speak to what's happening in our world or in the congregants' lives. I use this form of preaching regularly, though not typically drawing the text from the lectionary. Instead I'll preach through a book of the Bible, or the stories from the life of a biblical character, or a particular group of scriptures (the parables of Jesus, a certain category of Psalms, or the Ten Commandments, etc.)

But there is another way to approach preaching (I'll illustrate this for you nonpreachers in a moment): rather than starting with the answer then looking for the question or problem, we can start with the question or problem in the world or our hearers' lives, then search for the answer. (For preachers, we search for that answer in scripture.)

This requires identifying questions, concerns, and individual or communal problems, then exegeting (unpacking or seeking to understand) these. We study and consider the question or the problem, so that we can understand why it is our hearers are asking it, or facing it, or wrestling with it.

As an example, several years ago I surveyed the congregation I serve and discovered that a significant number of people were struggling with issues related to forgiveness. This led me to prepare a series of sermons on forgiveness. Each message started with the various problems our members had articulated to me regarding their struggles with forgiveness. I sought to "exegete" the various problems they had in forgiving others. Exegeting this meant trying to understand the various situations in which forgiveness was particularly difficult to offer or accept. Once I understood more about the problem, I was able to look for biblical texts offering insight, wisdom, and inspiration related to forgiveness. (This series was eventually published as a book called *Forgiveness* by Abingdon Press.)

In this kind of preaching, often called topical or thematic preaching, you start with the problem, study to gain clarity about it, then offer answers from scripture and illustrate those answers with real-life examples. The structure of this kind of preaching looks like this:

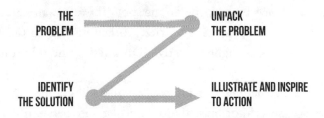

These two different approaches, starting with the problem or starting with the solution, apply to all kinds of presentations. Years ago a vacuum cleaner salesman came to our door. He didn't begin by telling us what a great vacuum cleaner he was selling. He began by asking if he could use our own vacuum cleaner to vacuum our carpets. We let him do this and he ran our vacuum over our living room carpet a couple of times. Then he said, "Now, I'd like to show you what's still down in your carpet." He plugged in his demonstration model, inserted a new filter, and vacuumed the same carpet. Then he opened up his cleaner and showed us what it had picked up. Yikes! We had a problem we did not even know about.

Once we were sold on the fact that our old vacuum cleaner wasn't getting the job done and that we had all kinds of dirt in our carpets that we could not see, he explained how his company's product was a superior vacuum cleaner, with more power and suction, leaving our carpets cleaner for our little daughter.

I had just graduated from seminary and we were too poor at the time to buy his vacuum cleaner. But if we'd had the money we would have bought one on the spot. The salesman started by showing us the problem and then worked his way to the solution, and it was highly effective. I'm guessing he sold a lot of vacuums.

Both structures can provide a compelling approach for a message, speech, or presentation, and I rotate between the two in the sermon series I deliver at the church I serve. My experience is that people are more often immediately engaged when the message begins with the question, problem, or issue, but both can be effective.

The starting point is a critical consideration in speaking well. Carefully determine which approach will work best: starting with the question or starting with the answer. Often, the question is the right place to start.

START

SAVVY SPEAKERS DETERMINE WHICH IS THE BEST STARTING POINT FOR THEIR TALK: THE QUESTION OR THE ANSWER. THEY OFTEN BEGIN WITH THE QUESTION OR PROBLEM, WHICH IMMEDIATELY ENGAGES THE AUDIENCE.

Chapter Four

INCLUDE THE KEY INGREDIENT

You've got great content. You feel passionate about your subject matter. You're clear about your why, who, and what. Your presentation is well researched. You seem to have all the makings for a great speech, talk, or sermon. Then you deliver your talk and you watch as your hearers' eyes start to glaze over. A week later (maybe sooner) no one can remember what you spoke about. What went wrong?

There's one ingredient that is vital to most effective talks: illustrations. Illustrations are usually stories, though they might be video clips or even photographs that illustrate the point you are trying to make in a way that touches the heart. Most of the time a presentation must move from the head to the heart if your hearers are going to remember it. It's no accident that the Gospel accounts of Jesus' teachings are loaded with his stories and other illustrations drawn from everyday life. Most of the stories

Jesus told are known as parables. Undoubtedly, Jesus taught far more than what is recorded in scripture—John tells us that all the books in the world could not contain it! But what his early disciples remembered were the stories he told to illustrate some dimension of what he called "the kingdom of God."

Those who speak well are constantly looking for great stories. I often carry a small moleskin notebook with me to write down things that happen to me or to those around me, or illustrations drawn from nature, so that I can later remember them and file them away for future sermons. As I read the daily news on my computer I regularly save stories in files that I think might illustrate a sermon or talk at some point in the future.

I've been to a half dozen shows on Broadway. I always take a pen and paper with me. I've found that every great play or musical deals with some dimension of the human condition. Most are packed full of illustrations. I do the same with movies. I enjoy the show, but sometimes, in the darkness, I get out my pen and write down some scene that illustrates a truth I'll be preaching about in the months ahead.

My children, as they were growing up, were a regular source of illustrations, though we had an agreement (drafted by my daughter, Rebecca) that I had to ask permission in advance to use something they said or did in a sermon or be fined five dollars per time I told the story! Even our animals provide great illustrations and stories. What makes these illustrations so effective is that they are the kind of everyday things that nearly everyone can imagine or relate to in some way, but that serve to illustrate a point in the message.

Here are a couple of examples of these kind of stories: On many occasions our beagle, Maggie, has served to illustrate my sermons. She's a great dog and we love her like crazy, but she does things that dogs do that perfectly illustrate our tendency as human beings to do things we should not do. Several years ago, while outside, she found what must have looked to her a bit like a black cat. This "cat" had a white stripe running down its back! Maggie decided she wanted to play. Soon she yelped and came running back to the back door, scratching to get in. We opened the door and she bounded inside and we knew instantly what had happened to her. We quickly grabbed her and put her back outside until we could figure out what to do. She could not come into our home until she'd been washed in a solution recommended by the Humane Society—a solution that neutralized the stench. I used this story, along with a picture of Maggie, to illustrate the Christian concept of sin, its allure and impact, and baptism as a sign of God's forgiveness.

My family used to have horses. We would muck out their stalls each day and pile the manure up near the barn. One day as I was emptying the wheelbarrow I noticed a wildflower growing right in the middle of the manure pile. I took a picture of it on my phone as it seemed a great illustration for a message I was preaching on how beautiful things can come out of the unpleasant things that happen in our lives. I entitled the message,

"Manure Happens." The sermon began by looking at the ubiquity of adversity and difficulty in life (point A) illustrated by examples from the Bible and from everyday life. Point B looked at how biblical characters had trusted God in difficult times and explored what it means for us to do the same. The final point of the message looked at how God uses these unpleasant and often painful experiences in our lives. Placed in his hands, he brings something beautiful from them. The photo drove the point home.

Sometimes I'll use a video clip from a film to illustrate a point in a talk. Our church purchases a license each year to cover our use of the film clips we use. There are a few rules of thumb I have for using film clips and most other uses of video: First, the ideal length of a clip is under two minutes—there are exceptions, but not many. In addition the audio from the clip must be clearly understandable when played back in the room I'm speaking in. Finally, when shown, someone who has not seen the rest of the film has to be able to get the point I'm trying to illustrate by the clip.

I find video interviews compelling as well. These can be very powerful. Once I interviewed a Holocaust survivor in her tailor's shop in Kansas City. She told the horrific story of her childhood under Nazism, showing the number tattooed into her forearm, then talking of the death of her family. But then she spoke of the importance of demonstrating love rather than revenge. She had the moral authority to say something like this and there wasn't a person in the room who was not affected by her story.

I've interviewed carpenters, shepherds, older adults, and children. Ask the right questions, get people talking, and often they will say things that are deeply moving, or which perfectly illustrate the point you are trying to make. These interviews do not require a film crew. If you have a smartphone, you can do this yourself. Frame your subject with a torso shot, slightly off center. Record a bit of footage of the person's hands, or of them doing something—pros call this "B-roll" and it is used to cover edits. Use a simple video editing program on your computer to add the B-roll and to trim up your clip, and add music or other sound if you want to. Or just record a single clip and use it as is.

At times I'll mention on Facebook what I'm speaking on and invite others to suggest illustrations or their own personal stories that illustrate the point. When I am desperate and can't find an illustration I'll visit www.preachingtoday.com, sponsored by *Christianity Today*. You can search by topic or theme to find dozens of stories and illustrations related to hundreds of topics. There's an annual fee to use the site, which is well worth it if you find several good illustrations a year.

A couple of final pointers: I've observed speakers whose entire talks were strings of interesting stories. People enjoyed the stories, but when the speaker was finished, no one was quite sure what the point was. Make sure you and your audience are clear about what the illustration is illustrating! One story per point is usually sufficient. If you have multiple stories for a single point, just choose the best one and leave the others out. And remember that what makes a good story a great illustration is delivery. Practice telling the story out loud to see what works best. Don't bog it down with too much detail, but include enough to fire up your audience's imagination. Practice your introduction to video illustrations too. Set them up so that people know what to listen for, but don't give away too much. Let the video speak for itself.

Speeches, talks, and sermons should nearly always include illustrations to touch people's hearts. Your hearers will remember key points if they connect on an emotional level. Use relevant stories from everyday life, including videos and photographs, to illustrate your message.

RELEVANT STORIES FROM EVERYDAY LIFE, SKILLFULLY TOLD, ARE THE ONE INGREDIENT YOUR SPEECHES, TALKS, OR SERMONS CAN'T DO WITHOUT.

Chapter Five
HUMOR ME

A fellow preacher once told me, "Once you make people laugh you can tell them anything after that." He was right. Human beings need, and like, to laugh. Laughter breaks up the tension. It warms up the crowd. So humor is often a great component to include in your opening remarks. Over the years, while attempting to ramp up my humorous speaking skills, I've bought joke books, searched humor websites, and asked my Facebook friends and Twitter followers for jokes that would help me with a talk. Now and then, I find a joke that's just right. But usually the best sources of humor are the situations and conversations going on around me every day. If you watch really funny people, much of their humor is not in the form of jokes, but stories from daily life.

I was preparing to speak about marriage and the way men and women don't often communicate well. I mentioned this on Facebook and invited friends to share humorous stories. A woman in our congregation wrote to say that her husband was doing the laundry one Saturday morning, wanting to wash his lucky college sweatshirt before sitting down to watch his team play. He hollered to her from the laundry room, "Honey, what temperature should I wash my sweatshirt at?" She asked, "What does it say on the sweatshirt?" To which he replied, "Kansas State!" This got a good laugh and it illustrated some differences between how men and women communicate. As noted in an earlier chapter, sometimes the most powerful illustrations are of a time when you have blown it. It's even better if the story is funny—something you and your audience can laugh at together.

Some years ago I was baptizing a child at our Sunday evening worship service. I was exhausted. It had been a busy week and I had already preached four services that weekend. As I prepared to baptize the child I invited the congregation to pray with me. I held the child in my arms, bowed my head, and prayed, "Lord, bless this food we are about to receive . . ," I stopped, realizing what I had just said, and the congregation broke out in laughter. The whole thing was recorded on video; it was quite embarrassing. When I speak on leadership at some conferences, where I want to break down barriers and gain a hearing, I'll invite the audience to watch a video clip of the baptism. I don't tell them what they are about to see; I only ask them to watch for the leadership principle illustrated by the video clip. The video clip elicits laughter from the audience, who is unprepared for my embarrassing faux pas. What's the leadership lesson in that botched baptism clip? Effective leaders don't take themselves too seriously, and they are willing to let others laugh at them. The reason I do this is that, after the clip, when the audience has had a chance to laugh at and with me, they always seem more open to hear everything else I'm about to share.

Keep a notebook or file where you write down humorous experiences from your own life or funny things you see or hear, so that you've always got a bit of humor to draw from. It's not critical to begin every talk with humor, but a funny story is often a great way to begin.

Humor is an important part of life—and important for speaking well. Pay attention to the people and circumstances around you, looking for humor in everyday life. Collect funny stories and jokes to share, usually near the beginning of your talks. And remember to laugh at yourself.

GOOD HUMOR IS IMPORTANT FOR ANYONE WANTING TO SPEAK WELL. SKILLFUL SPEAKERS PAY ATTENTION, LOOKING FOR HUMOR IN EVERYDAY LIFE. THEY USE FUNNY STORIES OR JOKES NOW AND THEN, ESPECIALLY NEAR THE BEGINNING OF THEIR TALKS. AND SOMETIMES THE JOKE IS ON THEM!

CROWD-SOURCE YOUR CONTENT

Facebook is one of my favorite tools for soliciting ideas for sermons and other talks. Most weeks I'll post a question related to the message I'm preparing and invite people, many of whom will be listening to the message, to give me their ideas, stories, input, or feedback. What a gift! I'll ask if anyone has insights on a particular scripture, or how they feel a scripture applies to their lives. I'll mention the central point of the sermon and ask if anyone has a great personal story that illustrates the point. If the information I'm requesting is too personal, I'll ask people to private message me their answers. I have had people share with me such moving personal stories and give me permission to share them provided I changed enough details that they would not be recognized.

At other times the information I receive from using social media is less dramatic but still interesting. As I was writing this chapter I posted the following on Facebook:

Today I'm hoping to finish a small little book with nineteen tips for preachers, teachers, and public speakers called *Speaking Well*. I'm curious what you think makes for a great sermon—what is it about an inspiring or effective sermon that makes it so? And when you hear a poor sermon, what made it poor?

Within an hour I had ninety responses, mostly people who are not clergy but who had definite ideas about what makes for effective or ineffective sermons. I looked for common threads and for points I hadn't thought of. This material will be useful for the talks I give on preaching, and most of the suggestions are included in this book. Interested in knowing what people on Facebook said? Here are a few actual responses to the question about what makes for a poor message:

"Rambling and never makes a point"

"Disconnected from the hearer's daily life"

"Lack of stories to illustrate points"

"Lack of passion and authenticity"

"Monotone presentation style—read the manuscript word for word"

"Boring!"

Some of the most pertinent and impactful stories I've used in sermons came from people responding to a Facebook query.

At times when I'm speaking at a conference I'll send a tweet as I'm preparing my talk, something like, "Preparing talk for xyz conference, participants what do u need to hear? #xyz." This allows me to hear brief questions or comments from those I'm speaking to as I'm preparing my talk. Some preachers will raise the caution, "Aren't you just tickling itching ears, telling them what they want to hear?" But my questions sent by social media are not "what do you want to hear?" but "what do you need to hear?"

Soliciting ideas and input from social media does not replace your research and study, but it does give you a vehicle for inviting hearers into the conversation before you speak, and it helps you to understand the needs, concerns, perspectives, and life experiences of your hearers.

Once a year I send an e-mail to my congregation inviting them to share their ideas for the coming year's sermons. I specifically ask these questions:

- If I were to preach a series of sermons that would be of interest to your friends who don't attend church, what would that series of sermons be about?

- What areas of the Bible, Christian theology, or the spiritual life would you like to grow in or know more about in the coming year? Are there theological or biblical questions you would like to hear a sermon tackle?

• What are the personal challenges and struggles you, or people you love, are facing?

I compile the answers to these questions and look for common trends in the congregation as well as fresh ideas, and these help me as I am planning the next year's sermons. I typically have a two-year sermon plan, though only the next twelve months are relatively firm (and even these are subject to change).

Finally there are times when I solicit more in-depth information from the congregation or those I'll be speaking to using Survey Monkey or other survey websites. The data is anonymous and easily compiled. Each time I preach on relationships, we invite the entire congregation to take a Survey Monkey survey. While we never get 100 percent participation, the last relationship survey had five thousand respondents, a statistically significant number. I could easily preach for several years on relationships based on the information gleaned from this survey! (This information and the sermons I preached on it are found in my book *Love to Stay*, published by Abingdon Press in 2013.) The statistics, information, and messages had a significant impact because they reflected the real-life relationship experiences of the people in the congregation. People came each week anxious to hear the results of the survey, how their personal experiences lined up against the survey data, and how the Bible might speak to their life situations.

The audience can actually be a vital source of material. Use all the means available to invite others to share stories, ideas, and feedback. This helps you to better understand your audience, and gives you material that is relevant to them. Use this crowd-sourced content in your speeches, sermons, or talks.

THE AUDIENCE CAN ACTUALLY BE A VITAL SOURCE OF MATERIAL. RESOURCEFUL SPEAKERS INVITE OTHERS TO SHARE STORIES, IDEAS, AND FEEDBACK FOR THEIR SPEECHES, SERMONS, OR TALKS.

Chapter Seven
DITCH THE EXTRA POINTS

Years ago I was listening to a friend preach, and, as I always do when listening to others speak or preach, I was taking notes. When he came to the end of his sermon, he had attempted to make fourteen different points (I was counting), fourteen ideas he felt were important that he wanted his audience to hear and retain. Most were really great points. But his message was ineffective for two reasons: (1) The congregation became lost in the flurry of ideas and began to tune out around point number four. (2) There was not nearly enough time to develop any of the fourteen points. There was no time to unpack the solution or answer each point raised. And there was certainly no time to share compelling and memorable illustrations or to inspire people to practice any of the points.

Speakers and preachers often denigrate the "three point" message. But there is a reason this idea took hold. Nearly everyone can remember three key points. This is particularly true if the points relate to each other, build upon one another, and are clearly connected. Using the idea from chapter 3, point A might lay out the problem, point B might demonstrate why the problem matters, and point C would offer a solution. Or, conversely, point A might offer a solution, point B would unpack this solution, and point C would make the case for the problem points A and B resolve. Ideally a three-point message or speech provides a logical progression of ideas, something like, A + B = C. Not every sermon I preach follows this pattern. At times I might lift up two or three separate points from a single text, demonstrating in each point of the message how the portion of the text I'm focused on in this one point provides an answer to a particular question or problem.

When a message has three distinct and only nominally related points, you should be able to answer this question: "If my hearers remember only one thing from this talk it should be . . ." Or, "What is the one thing I hope will change about people after they've heard my message?" Think of that one thing as something your audience will take with them when they leave your talk, the idea or conviction that will stick with them long after. Your sermon, message, or talk will be more compelling if you concentrate on the one thing (or at most the two or three things). Kelly Johnson, lead engineer at Lockheed's Advance Development Program in the mid-twentieth century, developed an acronym that reflected an engineering principle that applies to preaching and teaching: K.I.S.S. You no doubt remember this acronym: Keep It Simple Stupid, or sometimes, Keep It Short and Straightforward.

Simple and straightforward is far more effective and memorable in public speech than complex and convoluted. Read or recall public speeches that were powerful and memorable, and you'll notice that nearly all of them are centered on one distinct idea or one compact theme. I think of Churchill's brief but famous speech given to the Harrow School in October 1941. It was only eight paragraphs long. Yet people still remember and quote the speech to this day, and what they quote was the most compelling and simple of ideas, captured in the fourth paragraph of the speech.

Churchill was referring to Great Britain's stand against the Nazis in the face of the German Luftwaffe's "Blitzkrieg"—the air raids in which the Germans dropped over one hundred tons of bombs on Great Britain, destroying more than a million homes and killing more than forty thousand people. This was Churchill's central charge to the students: "Never give in, never give in, never, never, never—in nothing, great or small, large or petty—never give in except to convictions of honor and good sense. Never yield to force; never yield to the apparently overwhelming might of the enemy."[1] This speech was uncluttered and its takeaway was clear.

---

1. Winston Churchill, "Never Give In" (speech, Harrow School, Great Britain, October 29, 1941), http://www.winstonchurchill.org /resources/speeches/1941-1945-war-leader/never-give-in.

"Less is more" when it comes to the points you are trying to make as a speaker. Your talks will be more effective and will have greater impact if you focus on one central idea and give your hearers a simple, straightforward takeaway.

EFFECTIVE SPEAKERS CHOOSE ONE CENTRAL IDEA AND FOCUS ON THAT, GIVING THEIR HEARERS A SIMPLE, STRAIGHTFORWARD TAKEAWAY.

Chapter Eight
INVITE PARTICIPATION

When you are making a lengthy presentation (more than forty-five minutes), it is helpful to break up your talk by giving the audience a chance to actively participate. Typically this means asking people to answer a question or discuss a topic in the midst of your talk. This is harder to do effectively than it might seem. Some people do it masterfully, others not so well. A properly worded question or well-directed conversation will engage your audience. Poorly asked questions or poorly directed conversation only makes people uncomfortable. I've watched people who make their living delivering seminars leave people squirming when they ask questions that are unclear.

When I use this technique as I'm speaking at conferences, I'll ask questions at several junctures during my talks. It breaks up the time, injecting energy into the audience. It also gives people a chance to discover answers together or to apply what I've just taught. When speaking on leadership, I typically invite people to write down an answer to a question like, "What are three attributes or practices of a lousy leader?" I give them ninety seconds to answer this somewhat humorous question. Then I ask them to take two minutes to share and compare answers with one or two other people sitting near them. I note the half-way point in the conversation, then count down the last ten or fifteen seconds. I might ask for people to shout out some of their answers. Asking a clear question, giving people time to write down possible answers, then inviting them to discuss with each other allows valuable interaction between participants, adds energy to the group, and allows them to discover on their own things I'm about to teach.

After giving my hearers time to discuss the practices of a lousy leader, I might say, "Here's one of the most important things I can teach you about leadership: all the stuff on the list you just made, the practices of lousy leaders—DON'T DO THAT!" This solicits a laugh, so the audience is engaged in a positive way. Based upon this first list of the attributes of lousy leaders, I invite them to discuss the practices and qualities of effective leaders. What they quickly discover is that this list is a near exact opposite of the first list. As I describe the traits and practices of highly effective leaders they find that many of the things on my list, are on their list as well. The key is to do them.

This kind of conversation recognizes that people intuitively know much of the information you will share with them. I believe this kind of engagement fosters respect for the speaker because the speaker respects the audience enough to assume they know something about the subject matter.

What I've just described is a bit different than what many speakers do when inviting audience participation. Speakers often pose a question and then ask for immediate answers. When no one responds it becomes a bit uncomfortable. The speaker feels the need to rephrase the question, then waits again for responses. Few people like being put on the spot. If the questions are complicated or unclear, the awkwardness is compounded. Eventually someone responds, just to get things moving again! Instead of this rapid-fire question-and-answer technique, try giving people a couple of minutes to respond in silence, writing their answers down. Next let them share with people seated nearby. Then invite a few to share their responses aloud. And remember to keep your questions or conversation starters simple and lighthearted.

There are other ways of inviting the audience or congregation to participate. You may invite them to read something aloud that appears on a screen. You may ask them to complete a sentence from a statement or scripture that is familiar to all. I've invited audiences to join me in singing a familiar song. Provided it won't embarrass anyone, I will sometimes invite people to raise their hands if they have ever said, thought, or done a certain thing.

The aim of audience participation is usually engagement, but sometimes it can also be a way of illustrating a point. Several years ago I was speaking to a conference of about two thousand people of varying ages, but mostly people over sixty. I was trying to illustrate the point that the world is changing and organizations and churches must "change, innovate, and improve," or they will risk dying. I was illustrating this "the world is changing" point by examining the ways we access music. Nearly everyone in the room indicated that they enjoyed listening to music. I walked through the various ways people have accessed music in the last one hundred years—from LPs to 8-tracks to cassettes to CDs and finally through digital music players, including our phones. Next I asked how many people continued to listen to music primarily through LPs, cassettes, or CDs. About 70 percent of the audience raised their hands. Then I asked those who were under thirty-five to stand and I asked them the same question. The number of people who accessed music by CD or other forms of physical media was nearly zero. I then asked how many of this group access music primarily through their phone or other digital device and it was nearly 100 percent. It was a clear demonstration of the point that the world is changing and that change-resistant organizations will struggle to connect with future generations, but what made it particularly powerful was that it was the audience themselves who made the point—I wasn't reporting something I'd read somewhere. This was the experience of people sitting (and standing) in the room. Inviting the congregation to join you in a conversation with some give-and-take can be key to effectively communicating your point.

Sometimes, speaking well means allowing the audience to do the speaking. Simple, well-worded questions or conversation starters generate active participation, breaking up a long speech and fully engaging the audience.

USE SIMPLE, WELL-WORDED QUESTIONS OR CONVERSATION STARTERS TO GENERATE ACTIVE PARTICIPATION, BREAKING UP A LONG SPEECH AND FULLY ENGAGING THE AUDIENCE.

Chapter Nine

PUT A REMINDER IN THEIR HANDS

What if your audience remembered a message years after you delivered it? As we've learned, stories are one key. But another tool to help make this happen is to give people something tangible to take with them to remind them of your talk. Better yet, give them something that elicits an action and relates to your message. The kind of things I'm talking about are inexpensive but can have a big impact.

Let's start with something as simple as an outline of your talk with a place for hearers to take notes. I try to provide an outline when I speak at seminars and conferences. We provide this every week in our worship services and include daily scripture readings for the week ahead that tie back to the weekend message. Several times each year we put something more into people's hands. I recently arrived at a conference to speak, and no one was provided with pens or paper to take notes. I was going to offer a somewhat technical description of certain aspects of leadership. I believed this message was important and would help my hearers be more effective at their work. While I always take a notebook and pen when I'm going to hear a speaker, many people don't. If you want people to remember what you are sharing, provide them with an outline to take notes.

Sometimes we give people a small card printed with a statement to repeat throughout the week or a scripture verse to memorize. During a sermon series on the power of words we gave our members one of these containing two scripture verses, one on each side. I invited our people to say it every morning and every night for six weeks. I invited them to tape the card to their mirrors where they brush their teeth so they would remember the words long after the series was over. We repeated the passage aloud several times in each worship service too. The verse was Ephesians 4:29: "Let no evil talk come out of your mouths, but only what is useful for building up, as there is need, so that your words may give grace to those who hear" (NRSV). At the end of six weeks most of our congregation had memorized these words. That little card still hangs on a mirror in many of their homes, including mine!

One week I was preaching on the meaning of Christian baptism. At the end of the message I gave the congregation a prayer printed on a small plastic card with a rubber strap attached. I invited them to take this home and hang it in their showers and, as they entered the shower each morning, remember their baptism. The prayer reads, "Lord, as I enter the water to bathe I remember my baptism. Wash me by your grace. Fill me with your Spirit. Renew my soul. I pray that I might live as your child today and honor you in all that I do." This prayer reflected several of the things I'd taught our congregation about baptism. Eight years later I asked how many in our congregation still had these hanging in their showers and prayed the prayer daily. More than half raised their hands.

More recently I spoke on the Parable of the Sower (also known as the Parable of the Soils). In the parable Jesus describes the human response to his message by referring to seeds that fall on various types of soil: Some seed fell on the hardened soil and did not grow. The birds came and ate it. Some seed fell on shallow soil and it started to grow, but quickly died when the sun came out since the plants had shallow roots. Some seed fell among the thorns. The plant began to grow but was eventually choked out by the weeds. Some seed fell on good soil and it produced a harvest, thirty, sixty, or one hundred times what was sown.

After sharing the parable, I explored its meaning. What exactly is that extra-bountiful harvest? As I see it, and as I said in the message that day, the harvest is our intentional acts of kindness, compassion, love, justice, and witness—the things we do to bless others and to participate in God's work in the world. We considered what these might look like in our daily lives. Then I suggested that each person in our congregation aim to produce a one hundred-fold harvest—one hundred acts of kindness, compassion, love, justice, or witness over the course of a year. I set up the conclusion of the message, the call to action, by telling the people a story of what one pastor in our church did to connect with new people.

Scott Chrostek, a gifted young pastor on our team, set a goal for himself to connect with new people outside of our congregation. Scott put thirty-five pennies in his right pocket at the start of every day. Each time he had a conversation with someone unconnected to the church he moved a penny from his right pocket to the left. His aim was to move all the pennies by the end of each day. I asked the congregation to adopt a modified form of this habit as a way to intentionally practice kindness, encouragement, justice, or witness. At the end of this message, we gave each person a coin about the size of a silver dollar that read "The parable of the sower" on one side and "100 acts of kindness, encouragement, justice, and witness" on the other. Each day they were to be intentional about practicing at least one act of kindness, encouragement, justice, or witness. If they did they were to move the coin from one pocket to the other. If each person moved their coin once every three days, they would produce one hundred such acts in a year. I was confident they could achieve this. And sure enough, nearly a year later members regularly stop me, reaching into their pockets to show me their coins and share their stories of "being the harvest" by serving, blessing, and encouraging others.

Over eleven thousand people heard the message that day. If all of them accepted this challenge, they would produce 1.1 million acts of kindness, compassion, and witness over the course of the year. In a previous chapter, I urged you to answer the "So what?" in your talks, to give the audience a call to action or a way to respond. The little coins or tokens we gave out cost only pennies apiece, but they helped our people not only remember an important message, but to act on it.

Help your audiences to remember your messages by giving them a tangible reminder to take with them. Make it something that relates to your topic and elicits an action or response, and not only will your audience remember the talk, they'll be changed by it.

SPEAKERS MULTIPLY THE IMPACT OF THEIR TALKS WHEN THEY GIVE THE AUDIENCE A TANGIBLE REMINDER THAT RELATES DIRECTLY TO THE MESSAGE AND ELICITS AN ACTION OR RESPONSE.

SKIP THE SLIDES (OR AT LEAST USE THEM WELL)

I f you are a big presentation slides user I've got bad news for you. Many who sit in the audience believe that speakers who rely too heavily on presentation slides are masking the lack of content in the message or the speaker's ineffectiveness as a speaker. Graphics, photos, and video can be effective, as we'll see in the next chapter. But there are several reasons to minimize your use of text-based presentation slides.

As we've seen, eye contact, facial expressions, and hand gestures are all important aspects of your communication with an audience. The audience or congregation are not watching you or receiving the nonverbal information you communicate with your eyes and body, if they are watching words float across a screen. Even the slickest presentation slides are a poor substitute for you.

In addition, a host of things can go wrong when your message is overly dependent upon a slide presentation. You may arrive at your event only to find that the cable needed for your computer is not present. You may find there is no plug-in near the podium. The screen may be too small. The bulb could go out on the projector. You get the idea. On far too many occasions I've watched speakers labor with the technology of a presentation, getting flustered or irritated, while the entire audience mentally checks out. A technological failure and your response to it can completely undermine your talk and leave you a nervous wreck.

There are times when a good slide will help you communicate better. But I'd suggest not including all of your material—points, subpoints, and illustrations—on presentation slides. People should be looking at you during most of your talk. Use slides only to emphasize your key points, and limit the number of words on each slide.

Text on slides should closely reflect what you are saying. Don't force the audience to choose between listening to your words and reading completely different words on the screen. The slides should show the key phrases or words that you are speaking aloud. Using text on slides can be helpful for brief passages that you want the audience to say aloud or to write down.

I also use slides to give clear instructions for periods of active audience participation. For example, display a brief reflection and discussion question on screen as you invite the audience to write and then discuss their thoughts on a topic.

Give your presentation slides (and other graphics or video clips) to the media team as early as possible. When making arrangements for a speaking engagement, get the name and contact info for the person responsible for technical support, and communicate with that person in advance. Plan a time to walk through the presentation together at the event site.

Spend less time on your presentation slides and more time making sure your talk is great. Too often presenters seem to have spent more time adding cool effects to their slide show than preparing something worth saying. Finally, always make certain your talk works without the technology, and be prepared to deliver it that way!

SMART SPEAKERS USE TEXT-BASED PRESENTATION SLIDES SPARINGLY, AND ONLY TO EMPHASIZE KEY POINTS OR TO FACILITATE AUDIENCE PARTICIPATION.

Chapter Eleven

SHOW THE PICTURES

Text-based presentation slides can get in the way of speaking well, but at times visual images can be worth a thousand words. Images that illustrate your points can add emotional punch and layers of nuance to your talk, giving the audience more than just your words to remember. Photos, graphs, maps, timelines, and video clips are especially useful.

Photos are easier than ever to capture. Most of you reading this book probably have a smartphone with a built-in camera. You probably carry it with you nearly everywhere you go, so it's always handy. If you pay attention, you'll find frequent opportunities to snap a shot that perfectly illustrates a point. Our granddaughter recently turned one and, as is the tradition for many, her parents baked her a small birthday cake that was placed on the tray of her highchair. She spent thirty minutes digging her hands (and feet) into the cake, eating it, and getting chocolate icing all over her face, hair, hands, and feet. I snapped a picture and, with her mother's permission, shared it as a part of a message describing the simple things that bring us joy.

Graphs can also be helpful in illustrating a point. They help your audience to compare and contrast information, and they make sometimes-dry information easier to understand. Graphs work best when they illustrate a point dramatically—a significant one-year statistical jump, for instance. Graphs illustrating increments are almost always boring, tedious, and hard to read. Design your graphs to be bold, clear, and legible from the back row.

When I'm teaching about biblical events I often use maps to show where the event took place and timelines to show when the event occurred in the context of other biblical or world events. I use an iPad with a program that allows me to write on the slides, so I can show movements of people across a map or a timeline. When speaking about places your audiences has never been and events that are in the past, maps and timelines can be very helpful.

Video clips allow your audience to hear from other "voices" and travel to faraway places. They can add dimension, richness, and depth to your talks. I use them with some regularity. Interviews, sometimes called testimonials, can serve as powerful illustrations, as the person interviewed tells their own story related to the point. The audience connects emotionally with the "real person" in your clip, and thus they connect with your material. Adding music under the interview increases that emotional connection. Most computers now include a simple editing program, so you can do this yourself. As noted earlier, occasionally I use clips from movies, which are legally covered by a license we purchase each year at the church. Film clips can be very powerful, but, as also noted earlier, film clips are most impactful in a talk when the clip is no more than two minutes in length. Longer than this and the audience or congregation can forget where you were going in your talk. In addition, clips longer than this can sometimes drag.

Speaking well will often involve photos, graphics, and video, but excellent speakers understand that "less is more" when it comes to using visual images. Use short video clips and a few compelling visual images to make your talks stronger and more effective.

EXCELLENT SPEAKERS UNDERSTAND THAT "LESS IS MORE" WHEN IT COMES TO USING VISUAL IMAGES. SHORTER VIDEO CLIPS AND FEWER BUT MORE COMPELLING VISUAL IMAGES MAKE A STRONGER AND MORE EFFECTIVE TALK.

GET THE LITTLE THINGS RIGHT

I t's often the little things in life that make the difference, isn't it? For speakers, the "little things" relate to the mechanics of the task—microphones, wardrobe, lighting, and other details. Put in the time and effort to master these, and your speaking will be less stressful, more rewarding.

A small thing like a microphone, or even a battery, can have big consequences when you are speaking. I was once speaking to about two thousand people at a conference when in the midst of my talk the batteries went dead on my lavaliere microphone pack. Suddenly something as small as two AA batteries temporarily ended my talk and when, three minutes later, I had new batteries installed, the interruption had a significant negative impact on my presentation. Now I always check the battery level before I get up to speak or I ask those running sound if they can provide a fresh battery before I begin.

Speaking of microphones, give yourself extra time to get your mic on and secured. When using a lavalier mic (one that clips to your clothing) make sure it is in the right position and then tuck the wire inside your clothing—under your shirt or around the back of a jacket. Don't leave the wire hanging out, which will look sloppy and unprofessional to many in the audience.

Over-the-ear mics (often referred to as a Countryman mic, after the brand that popularized them) are increasingly popular among sound technicians. They provide more consistent sound, since they move with your head. But it can be tricky to fit these over-the-ear mics to your ear and face. Improperly placed, the mic can slip off of your ear in the middle of a talk. Or the little arm that runs from your ear across your cheek, placing the mic near your mouth, can swing and sway disrupting the sound. I almost always spend five or ten minutes fitting this type of mic to my ear and face. Here's a tip: Use clear medical tape, the kind you can buy for two dollars at the drug store, to tape these kind of mics to your face near your ear, securing it in place. Then tape the wire running off the back of your ear to your neck. The mic should be fixed and should not come loose. Finish by tucking the wire down the back of your clothing and run it to your battery pack. The sound technicians may not have this tape handy, so I take a roll of it with me wherever I am speaking. A two-dollar roll of medical tape can make all the difference in both peace of mind and in sound quality as you are speaking.

Get to know the names of the people who are running sound and video or graphics for your presentation. Connect with them prior to the event, if possible, and ask to meet with them at least forty-five minutes before your talk (earlier if possible) so that you can get mic'd up and they can test your mic's audio levels, as well as any photos and video clips you're using. Also walk them through the manuscript so they're comfortable with your cues. Make sure you have a podium, pulpit, or music stand to speak from. Check the lighting levels (more on that below). And make sure you have room temperature water within reach. (Cold water restricts throat passages). This will bring peace of mind for you and for the technical team.

Another tip is to carry all the various adapters you might need when using audio-visual materials. And it's a good idea to bring multiple formats of any clips or images you're using. Recently I was speaking at a large conference in Denver. I was planning on using my iPad for part of the presentation, but when I arrived the technical team did not have the exact adapter needed. Fortunately I had one in my backpack, and we were able to get the iPad hooked up and running, otherwise we would have been out several important graphics.

It's important to dress appropriately for the events where you are speaking. Ask well in advance how the audience or congregation will be dressed. You don't want your clothes to get in the way of your message, and if you are dressed too differently from the audience, your wardrobe can become a distraction.

If feasible, carry a change of clothing with you, either more or less dressy than the clothing you plan to wear. A couple of years ago I was asked to speak at a small liberal arts college. I asked, "What should I wear?" and the man helping me suggested I wear a suit and tie. I showed up and didn't see another soul wearing a tie, and certainly no suits. I quickly ducked into a bathroom, took off the tie, and switched my suit pants out for a pair of jeans.

Why does your clothing matter? Because many people decide in the first few minutes of seeing you, before you've spoken a word, whether they are going to give you a hearing. Your wardrobe should convey that you understand and are in sync with your audience.

Another of the important "little things" is the lighting on the area where the speaker stands. When the light on the speaker is dim, or even the same level as the light in the rest of the room, the speaker must work harder to gain and hold the audience's attention. Facial expressions and hand gestures are lost. The talk feels lower in energy when the speaker is poorly lit. If during your pre-speech walk-through with the technical team you see that the lighting is inadequate, ask the technician to raise it.

Pay attention to the "little things" in advance. Communicate in advance with the technical team so everyone knows what to expect. Arrive early, and bring with you any equipment or supplies you may need. The mechanical, technical, and environmental details can trip up any speaker, but a little time spent in preparation will result in a better presentation for your audience and less stress for you.

SPEAKING WELL REQUIRES ATTENTION TO THE "LITTLE THINGS" IN ADVANCE. WELL-PREPARED SPEAKERS ATTEND TO THE SMALL, TECHNICAL, AND ENVIRONMENTAL DETAILS, GAINING PEACE OF MIND FOR A SMOOTH, COMPELLING PRESENTATION.

Chapter Thirteen
WRITE IT OUT

One of the questions speakers have to wrestle with is whether to speak from a manuscript or an outline. Each method has its benefits, and I've done both. In my experience, outlines can be an important step in preparing a speech or sermon, but when it comes to actually giving the talk, ninety-nine times out of one hundred I'll be doing it from a manuscript.

The process of writing a manuscript helps me to clearly articulate each point. The act of writing the message out requires me to clarify and focus my points before actually sharing them with others. It forces me to articulate the transitions I will make from one point to the next. It allows me to see exactly how much time I am spending on each point. And it shows me how long the message will be. (I use Arial 11-point text, single spaced, and I've come to know that it takes about six minutes to deliver one page of text.) When I'm finished with the manuscript I can tell precisely how long the message is, whether I'm dwelling too long on one point, and where my transitions need work.

A manuscript also helps to keep me from "chasing rabbits." It acts as a kind of railing that keeps me on track as I'm speaking. Without a manuscript, speakers may be tempted to go on long detours (and sometimes get lost!). A manuscript is also a tremendous help when incorporating audio-visual elements in my message, particularly where someone else is controlling what appears on the screens. Each weekend I give a copy of my sermon manuscript to the video control team. They follow along and see exactly when to put up a quote or an image, or when to run a video clip.

I've also found the manuscript helpful for persons who are hearing impaired. Some years ago I asked our hearing-impaired members how I could better serve them and they indicated that it would be helpful to have a manuscript to read while I was preaching. It was actually this need that led me to start preaching by manuscript.

Finally, the manuscript creates a written record of what I preached or spoke about. This is particularly helpful if there is a story or a point that I think might be helpful when speaking in another location or to a different group. I'm able to pull up these stories and drop them into a new manuscript.

Every speaker needs a tool for delivering the talk—an outline or manuscript of some sort. The outline is a good step in the preparation process, but a full manuscript holds distinct advantages as a tool for delivery in speaking well. Spend the time to develop and memorize a manuscript, and your speaking will be more focused, with fewer detours, and you'll be more likely to stay on time.

A COMPLETE MANUSCRIPT KEEPS THE SPEAKER FOCUSED, ON TRACK, AND ON TIME.

Chapter Fourteen
SAY IT WITH YOUR EYES

I fell in love with my wife because of her eyes. I can instantly tell how she is feeling by looking into her eyes. They light up a room when she is happy. My kids say that lightning flashes from them when she's irritated! She doesn't have to say a word. Her eyes do all the talking.

When it comes to speaking well, eye contact is critical. I've known people, often authors, whose speeches had great content but their talks were horrible because they simply read their manuscript. I was recently at a seminar where people walked out before a speaker was finished because he just stood there and read from his manuscript, with virtually no eye contact or expression. This is one potential downside to using a manuscript. Some people feel so bound to their manuscript they find themselves stuck reading aloud.

I typically write four drafts of my sermons, with each one

further tweaking, tightening, and strengthening the manuscript. By the time I've written two or three drafts, I have the sermon or talk memorized. I keep the manuscript before me on the podium or pulpit when I speak, and I turn the pages along the way, but seldom look at it. It is there when I am quoting scripture or a source, but otherwise I'm only glancing at it from time to time to make sure I'm not forgetting anything and to help those who may be supporting my talk with video clips or quotes on the screen.

You've likely heard someone quote, or misquote, psychologist Albert Mehrabian's research that body language (posture, hands, and facial expressions) is responsible for 55 percent of the effectiveness of a speaker. Voice intonation was responsible for 38 percent of a speaker's effectiveness, and the speaker's words were responsible for only 7 percent of the speaker's effectiveness. Mehrabian's findings were a bit more nuanced than this. The subjects in his study were asked about *their feelings* in response to seeing and hearing someone speak. This is not exactly the same as how much information they retained or how close the presentation came to accomplishing its goal. Nevertheless, this research gives insight on how to engage an audience in a way that results in positive feelings toward the speaker and the presentation.

Mehrabian's work highlights what we know from our own daily interactions with other people: how we say something—our eyes, our facial expressions, our posture, our hands, and our tone of voice—plays a significantly greater role than our words do in how we will be heard and received by others, including our audiences or congregations.

SPEAKING WELL INVOLVES FAR MORE THAN THE WORDS WE USE. THE EYES, HANDS, FACE, POSTURE, AND TONE OF VOICE HAVE IT!

Chapter Fifteen
ANSWER THE "SO WHAT?"

The professor of my college preaching class told the story of an old preacher who came to realize that his preaching was having little impact. He recognized that while his preaching was generally interesting and delivered with conviction, he routinely failed to ask anything specific of his congregants. And so they seemed largely unchanged by his sermons. This was a rare and important insight. The preacher took a sheet of paper and wrote two words in huge letters across the page. He taped the paper to the top of the pulpit, where his sermon manuscript was meant to lay. Every week when he concluded his sermon and picked up his manuscript, he would see these two words, words that formed the question he felt he must be able to answer at the end of each sermon: SO WHAT?

Great speeches, sermons, and talks have a clear answer to the question "So what?" That answer is clear not only to the speaker but to the listeners as well. They should know what you are asking of them or have a clear idea of how they can and should respond to the message. The "So what?" is usually a specific call to action. In sales this is called asking for the sale or simply "the ask." I sold women's shoes in a high-end department store while in college. Women loved to come in and try on five, six, and sometimes seven pair of shoes. Then they'd say, "Thank you, I'm going to think about it." This had happened over and over, when a seasoned salesman pulled me aside and told me, "You've got to ask for the sale. Whichever of the shoes she seemed most interested in, ask if you can ring them up for her. You'll find when you do, she'll often say yes. She's waiting for you to ask."

I often hear speeches or sermons that end without the speaker ever giving "the ask." If the talk was good and compelling, then I want to do something about it, to take the next step or respond in some way. When no clear call to action is issued, I want to stand up and ask the preacher or speaker, "What do you want me to do in response to your message?"

Harry Emerson Fosdick was one of the great preachers of the first half of the twentieth century. He taught preaching at Union Theological Seminary in New York, but he also taught speaking at Columbia University's law school. He taught law school students and seminary students alike, that when he preached he imagined the Riverside Church where he served was a courtroom and the congregation was the jury. He envisioned himself as a prosecuting attorney, or a defense attorney, making the best case he could for the sermon's key theological, moral, or biblical idea. At the end of the message, he would give his closing arguments and pointedly ask the congregation for the verdict he was preaching toward. When I preach I often imagine the congregation in this way and seek to offer as persuasive a "case" and "closing argument" as possible. Then I ask them for a decision or course of action following the message. Fosdick's example is helpful for secular speakers too. If you hope to effect any sort of change as a result of your speaking, then it's just as important for you to answer the "So what?"

Your speaking will have the greatest impact when you directly ask the audience to do something, to take a next step, or to make a change. Consider the purpose of your speech, talk, or sermon—the why, who, and what—and give your audience a meaningful way to respond.

GREAT PREACHERS AND SPEAKERS GIVE A CLEAR ANSWER TO THE QUESTION "SO WHAT?"

Chapter Sixteen
ADDRESS THE HOT TOPICS

Politicians, preachers, teachers, and others are faced regularly with the challenge of speaking on controversial issues. What makes an issue controversial, among other things, is that a significant number of people understand and interpret the issue differently, and the issue stirs deep emotions for people on both sides.

When preaching, speaking, or teaching on these issues it is particularly important for the speaker to identify his or her goal. I'll put the question bluntly: Is your goal in speaking on a particular controversial issue merely to irritate or inflame or is it to influence? It's easy to irritate or inflame members of your audience or congregation. It takes no tact, little skill, and not much research to express your opinions on an issue in a way you believe is convincing, but that manages to alienate half of your hearers. To influence people so that they see things differently—that takes skill and a good deal of homework.

Audiences become most frustrated when a speaker addresses a controversial issue and misrepresents the views of others, or is dismissive of opposing views, or overstates their own views without acknowledging the shortcomings of those views. Here's what I've learned, sometimes the hard way, about speaking on controversial subjects:

First, always treat with respect those who hold opposing views. Take the time to read and fully understand their perspectives and their reasoning. Consider the most compelling case they themselves make for the position they hold. Be able to articulate that view as though it were your own. And find positive things to affirm about that view and/or those who hold it. There have been times when, after carefully studying the opposing view on an issue, I have understood the issue differently and modified my own view.

Second, thoroughly examine your position—the arguments for it and against it. Be willing to acknowledge its shortcomings and you'll find those who hold opposing views to be more likely to give you a hearing. Remove any barbs or incendiary words as you present your side of an issue. The labels used in debating an issue are often designed to elevate one's own views while denigrating the opponents' position.

When I preach on these issues I often devote the first one-third of my talk to making the case for one side of the issue, doing so with conviction and passion as though I were articulating my own view. Then I'll devote the next one-third of my talk to articulating the case for the opposing viewpoint. Again, I seek to articulate this view with knowledge, passion, and conviction.

My hope is that, after hearing the first two-thirds of the message, all hearers, regardless of which side of the issue they fall upon, could say that I've captured what they believe and why. At this point I also hope they have heard me express something positive or affirming about each side in the debate. By the time I begin my final one-third of the message people on either side are uncertain which view is my own, but they do know that I understand why they believe what they believe. In the last one-third of the message, I articulate, with humility (while giving permission to my hearers to disagree), my own views on the subject and why I hold them.

That may sound "weak" to some, but here's what I've seen over twenty-five years of addressing difficult subjects: This approach allows me to influence people rather than simply irritate them. It allows me to model an alternative to the increasingly divisive ways hot topics are discussed. And it opens the way for people to understand each other better—even, sometimes, to change their minds. People come to me after these talks and say things like, "I thought my views on this topic were settled. But listening to you helped me think about it differently. I can't believe it, but my views have changed."

Most groups are far more diverse than we might believe. A friend of mine pastors a church that is widely considered to be entirely "progressive" or "liberal." But I'd guess that 25 percent of his congregation watches Fox News and would consider themselves theologically and socially conservative. A member of a conservative congregation in my city once told me he was frustrated by his pastor's frequent preaching against homosexuality. The preacher must have assumed everyone in the congregation agreed with him, but the man clearly did not agree with his preacher on this issue. He was conservative in many ways, but his friendship with a gay coworker had left him uncomfortable with his pastor's preaching and unwilling to invite friends or coworkers to church. Be careful not to assume that your audience is of one mind.

If you are speaking to a group that shares common convictions about the controversial topic you are addressing (i.e., you are speaking on the importance of the Second Amendment to an NRA convention) your approach may be different. In that case, you are "preaching to the choir." But if you are speaking to a diverse group of people who hold differing opinions, your task is to understand the convictions and motives on both sides of the issue.

People interpret controversial issues differently, and there is often some truth in each perspective. If you hope to influence an audience, rather than irritate or inflame them, you should treat those on either side with respect, offer your convictions with humility, then explain the reasons for those convictions. And, if you can, acknowledge the possibility that you don't have all answers and may even be wrong. By taking this approach you increase the likelihood that you will not irritate but will actually influence your hearers.

?!?!

WISE SPEAKERS ADDRESS HOT TOPICS WITH CAREFUL STUDY, RESPECT FOR OPPOSING VIEWPOINTS, AND HUMILITY.

Chapter Seventeen
PUT YOUR HEART IN IT

S ome years back a friend called early one morning and said, "You've got to turn on the television, NOW!" I asked, "Why? And what station?" She replied, "You'll see, just turn on any local station," and then she hung up. Her message was short and didn't make any sense, but because of the urgency in her tone of voice and the fact that she was on the verge of tears, I knew I had to do what she said. I turned on the television to see the first World Trade Center with smoke and flames billowing from it.

Tone of voice plays an important part in effective speaking. This can vary from the lighthearted to the extremely urgent, as with my friend's phone call. My sermons often start with a bit of humor, and my tone is lighthearted. As I move into expounding a scripture or some dimension of the human condition—a problem, question, or concern—I move to teaching, and my tone becomes more direct and straightforward. My cadence is a bit quicker and more uniform. When I come to the solution and the call to action, my tone of voice changes. I project my sense of urgency, conviction, or passion—often it is this more urgent, passionate speech people refer to as "preaching."

I've noticed in speaking week after week that, while people appreciate the teaching portion of the sermon where the groundwork is laid, it is in the urgent, passionate preaching that people are most visibly moved. In this part of the sermon my voice rises slightly and my cadence quickens or slows down to emphasize the meaning of my words. My body language also changes—I'll step away from the podium and come closer to the congregation, leaning in to convey the importance of the point.

In this kind of preaching the entire body is used. Pauses and cadence changes give you a chance to take deep breaths, and your diaphragm allows you to control your breathing, giving your words power. Muscles in your abdomen, legs, chest, and arms all are used to help your body convey the point. Use them with intention—don't mindlessly wander, shuffle, or rock back and forth. You put all of your energy, and use your entire self in this kind of public speaking.

I preach five times each weekend and at the end of a weekend where I've thrown myself into preaching with this kind of passion, my abdominal muscles, arms, and legs are sore. I've thrown everything I've got into conveying the message. This kind of impassioned speaking comes from my utter conviction that what I am saying is true and that it really matters, or should matter, to my hearers.

Some years ago a preacher told me, "People come to church to see the preacher's convictions." This is not the only reason people come to church, but his point was a good one.

We are moved when we see and hear another person express with urgency their convictions. This emotional connection gives a speaker the power to influence change in others, for when we are moved we are more likely to change in some way. Put all your energy, your entire self, into your speeches, talks, or sermons, and your speaking will have this power.

EFFECTIVE SPEAKERS PUT THEIR WHOLE PERSON INTO THEIR SPEECHES OR SERMONS. THE TONE AND TEMPO OF THEIR VOICE VARIES AS THEY SPEAK; THEIR ARMS, HANDS, AND POSTURE ALL WORK TOGETHER TO CONVEY THEIR CONVICTIONS AND THE URGENCY OF THEIR MESSAGE.

Chapter Eighteen
EAT, PRAY, SLEEP

We're nearing the end of this little book, but there are several last important bits of counsel I would like to offer you about speaking well. These seem self-evident, but even seasoned public speakers, teachers, and preachers sometimes forget them, to their peril.

I was speaking at a conference recently. I gave my first talk on a Friday night. It ended about 9:30 p.m. I then met with young clergy for another ninety minutes, until 11:00 p.m. When I got back to my hotel I needed to write the weekly e-mail that goes out to my congregation. I finished at 1:00 a.m. Then I decided to respond to e-mail and Facebook messages. I finally fell into bed at about 2:30 a.m. Four and a half hours later my alarm went off. I got cleaned up, packed my bags, and went back to the conference to deliver my next ninety-minute plenary session.

There was no time for breakfast. I grabbed half a glass of sweetened iced tea and a cookie.

I'm hoping most didn't notice the effects of this on my talk, but I did. Here's what happened: I forgot several of my points. I lingered too long on others. My talk ran over by seven minutes. I didn't have the energy I usually have, and toward the end there were several moments when my speech was slurred. No, I hadn't been drinking. In fact, the problem was, I hadn't been eating, sleeping, or drinking properly. Your body needs rest. You are at your best when you've had a good night's sleep. The two thousand people at this particular conference got less than they should have from me because I failed to take care of myself.

You can have the best material and be well prepared (my talk for this conference was time tested and contained some excellent material), but if your body has not had adequate sleep, fluids, and nutrients, you'll not be your best. Make it your standard practice to get at least seven hours of sleep before speaking at an important event (which includes, for you preachers, getting to bed early on Saturday nights in preparation for Sunday worship). Eat a nutritious breakfast. Drink plenty of fluids. These simple practices are essential to effective speaking.

Two other practices seem self-evident, but even preachers often miss them: speakers need to make adequate time in their lives for prayer and reflection. This book is intended for a broad audience of speakers, and I've not focused on things like biblical exegesis and other forms of research in preparing one's message. There are a host of books that teach those practices. I've focused instead on the essential skills for *speaking* well. In order to prepare and then deliver excellent messages, it is essential for a speaker to have time to think about and reflect upon the ideas that will go into a speech or sermon. And it is essential to spend time praying and inviting God to guide, lead, and speak to you.

Reflection takes time, and the practice often gets crowded out of our busy lives. But taking the time to mull over points, to pray and meditate, and to study always results in deeper, more well-developed messages. Use your reflection time to read what others have written on a subject. Look for the latest research you can find on the topic or what commentators have written about it. If you're a preacher, study several different biblical commentaries (see the "Postscript for Preachers" for suggested resources). This brings new ideas and fresh insights. I often find during long walks as I'm pondering an upcoming talk or sermon, that I have a flash of insight, or I suddenly see some connection I'd not seen before. This is far more likely to happen when I've spent time reading and studying and praying. Once again this is why it is good to always carry a pen and small notebook, so that when you have such an insight you can write it down. Great preachers often note that their messages need time to "percolate." They make the time to reflect and think, and they put themselves in places where their creativity is stimulated.

And that leads to the idea of prayer. Some of you reading this book may not be people who pray much. But here's what I find when I'm praying about a message: I'm inviting God, who is the source of all wisdom, to speak to me and through me. I pray for the audience or congregation to whom I will be speaking. If I have a chance, I visit the auditorium or sanctuary where I will be speaking and walk through the rows of seats praying for those who will sit in these seats. I'll sit in one of the seats and as I do I thank God for the chance to speak to the people who will sit in this room. I ask God to use me to bless and encourage my hearers. Prayer is such a regular part of my weekly sermon preparation. As a preacher my aim, with fear and trembling in my heart, is to speak on behalf of God—I hope to be an instrument through which God speaks. To do that I've got to spend time listening for God, which is part of what happens in prayer, meditation, and study. As I pray, I give thanks to God, offer myself to God, and invite God to use me. Then I spend time in quiet, listening as I walk, read, and think, trusting that God might just speak through that "still small voice" of the Spirit, offering an insight, an application, or a timely word for the people to whom I will speak. This is the essence of inspiration: to be moved—inspired—by an idea or insight that is fresh, that seizes the imagination, the heart, and the mind leading to action. Whether one is a preacher, or a teacher, or a business leader, your audience is hoping for inspiration, and it is in prayer, listening, study, and meditation that this kind of inspiration comes.

Great material and thorough preparation are important, but if you neglect your own physical and spiritual well-being, you will fall short of your best as a speaker. Develop healthy habits to make sure you are nourished in every way, and your speaking will be more effective and satisfying.

EAT, PRAY, SLEEP, AND LISTEN. THESE ARE THE REGULAR PRACTICES OF EFFECTIVE SPEAKERS.

Chapter Nineteen

DELIVER THE MOST IMPORTANT MESSAGE

Okay, for this last chapter and the postscript that follows, I want to speak specifically to preachers, but if you're not a preacher, I suspect this last bit of advice will be pertinent to you as well. It's about integrity and who you are when you step off the stage or out of the pulpit. Here's the point in a nutshell: THE MOST IMPORTANT SERMON YOU'LL GIVE, IS THE SERMON YOU LIVE.

I have a confession: I haven't always practiced what I preach when I step into the pulpit. Sometimes my most powerful sermons are the ones I am delivering first to myself, the sermons *I* need to hear. But I make it my aim to never preach something to others that I don't intend to practice when I step out of the pulpit.

One of Jesus's great frustrations with the religious leaders of his day was that they did not practice what they preached. He repeatedly called them out, "How terrible it will be for you legal experts and Pharisees! Hypocrites!" The word *hypocrite*, in Jesus's day, meant an actor on a stage pretending to be someone they were not. I don't want to pretend to be something I am not—to be a play actor on a stage when I preach. I don't want to be a pretender.

I remember a professor in college (it may have been seminary; I've forgotten who said it, but the statement has stuck with me) once saying, "You can't lead people where you are not going." In addition I've found that people are regularly watching to see the sermon you live. They look to see how you drive. They watch to see how you treat other people when you are frustrated, or when someone else is frustrated with you. People see, and talk about, the sermon you live.

I often fail at perfectly living the Christian life. But it is my aim, every day as I begin the day, to live what I say I believe and what I teach others. I want to be not only a "hearer of the word" but "a doer also."

John's Gospel begins by describing Jesus as "the Word" and notes, "The Word became flesh and made his home among us" (1:14) The theological term for this idea is *incarnation*—a word that literally means "enfleshment." Jesus enfleshed or incarnated God's word to the human race. We who are his followers are called to continue this work of incarnating God's message to the world around us. It is as we seek to live the gospel that we find the insights and experiences that allow us to proclaim the gospel with conviction and power. It is then that our message becomes truly authentic. It is in this nexus of living and proclaiming, of deed and word, that we find the highest expression of speaking well.

THE MOST IMPORTANT SERMON YOU WILL EVER GIVE IS THE SERMON YOU LIVE.

Postscript for Preachers

RESOURCES FOR PREPARING EXCELLENT SERMONS

While this book has focused on a broader audience, I'm hopeful that many of its readers are preachers. And while I did not talk about biblical exegesis in the previous chapters, I'd like to say a few words about it here and to offer some of the resources I've found most helpful in my weekly work of preparing sermons.

Exegesis is literally the drawing out of the meaning of a text, and here we are talking specifically about biblical exegesis. It involves a careful study of the particular biblical text one might be preaching from, starting with the attempt to understand who the biblical author was writing to, the situation they may have been trying to address in writing what they wrote, and, by a careful study of the context and the words used in the original language in which it was written, what was meant by the text.

Translators have attempted to make the meaning clear when they translate the biblical text from its original language (Hebrew and a bit of Aramaic in the Old Testament, Greek in the New Testament). But the translated text doesn't tell us about the historical context of the passage or what can be deduced about who the text was originally written for and why. This is where study Bibles and commentaries help.

I begin my study of a text with prayer, inviting God to speak to me as I study. I'll then read the text I'm preaching on from several different translations. I might write down initial insights as well as questions from the text. I may at this point look to the original languages the text was written in by turning to a website like Bible Hub (www.biblehub.com) where I can look at the meaning of each Greek or Hebrew word in the passage. This may open up new insight into the meaning that I may not have seen before.

Though I have dozens of Bibles, I typically turn first to *The CEB Study Bible* and *The NIV Study Bible*. Both have excellent introductions to each book, cross-references, maps, study notes, and timelines. *The CEB Study Bible* leans toward mainline scholarship; *The NIV Study Bible* leans toward conservative scholarship. In this way they complement one another. In addition to the Common English Bible (CEB) and New International Version (NIV) translations, I make use of the New Revised Standard Version (NRSV). There are others I'll look at but these are where I start.

I usually go to the Bible Hub website to review the Hebrew, Aramaic, or Greek text from which the translators have done their work. There you can click on each word in the verse to see the Hebrew, Aramaic, or Greek word that lies behind the English. Clicking on that word will allow you to see how else this word is translated in the Old or New Testament, allowing you to see other possible meanings of the text.

I sometimes break the text up, diagramming a verse, or outlining a passage. If it is a Gospel passage and there are parallels to the passage in other Gospels, I'll read each of the versions of the passage and note their differences. I begin asking how this text might speak to our lives today. I try to draft a basic outline of what the passage might mean for my congregation and how it speaks to us today, before turning to the commentaries.

Twenty-five years ago I asked our congregation for continuing education funds each year to purchase books and resources to help with the year's sermons. Each year I add to my commentaries and other tools, and after twenty-five years I've been able to amass a library with excellent commentaries. I will usually start with commentaries like *The New Interpreter's Commentary* because its writers tend to draw upon the insights from most of the best commentaries produced in the decades leading up to its publication.

Increasingly I'm purchasing digital versions of commentaries or access to them on sites like Ministry Matters (www .ministrymatters.com), so that I can read and study even when

I'm out of town. Though I have many of the newer and more scholarly commentaries, I also still appreciate some of the older commentaries when it comes to connecting the Bible to daily life. *William Barclay's Daily Study Bible*, for example, despite its age and nonscholarly approach, is helpful in connecting the text to life. When it comes to archaeological and historic data, I've found the *Zondervan Illustrated Bible Backgrounds Commentary* on both the Old and New Testaments to be full of great historical information.

Among the other commentary series that I often turn to are the *Anchor Yale Bible Commentaries*, *The New International Commentary on the New Testament* and *The New International Commentary on the Old Testament*, the *Zondervan Exegetical Commentary on the New Testament*, and the series, *Interpretation: A Bible Commentary for Teaching and Preaching*. These are a mix of mainline and evangelical commentaries, and though the individual volumes vary in quality, I've found them to be helpful as a whole. I've also found the resources at www.textweek.com to be helpful. The commentaries and articles there are arranged according to the New Revised Common Lectionary, but they also have an index where you can search for a particular text and then find commentaries, articles, and illustrations built around the text. There are a host of other resources I'd love to mention, but this is only a postscript of a short book, and my aim is just to get you started.

The commentaries will often offer background information and connections of one text to another, that you might not have discovered on your own. Usually by the time I'm done studying the commentaries I've had a few more new insights into the text and the author's aim in writing it that have given me a few more ideas about how it might connect to my, and my congregation's, daily life.

As noted earlier in the book, I then began answering the questions why? who? and what? I think about the question the text answers or the problem for which it offers a solution, or how it points to some dimension of the human condition. I often ask, "What does this passage tell me about God? About humanity? About God's will for me?" During this phase, as with each that I've mentioned above, I devote some time to praying and listening for God.

Once I've begun to answer these questions, and I've got some idea of the two or three ways in which the text speaks to our lives, I start looking for illustrations. This may be, as described earlier, by asking questions on Facebook. It may be looking at my own life and experiences in ministry. I may think of an interview we might want to conduct to illustrate the message. Or I may have a film clip in mind. If I'm stuck and I don't have any illustrations, I will turn to the Preaching Today website (www.preachingtoday .com), which includes a vast archive of sermon illustrations that can be searched by theme or scripture verse.

It is helpful at times to see how other preachers have approached a particular theme or scripture text. There may be something they've seen that you've missed, or an illustration that would be helpful. This should not supplant your own research and you should not attempt to preach someone else's sermon, but it can help you when you are feeling stuck or give you an insight you might have missed. If you use something original from another's sermon, note this in your message with something like, "Jane Smith, in her sermon on this text, said . . ."

Church of the Resurrection has archived video and audio files (but not written manuscripts) of most of my sermons since 1999 at http://www.cor.org/worship/sermon-archives/. We are in the process of adding the ability to search for sermons by scripture, title, theme, and key word. When preaching on a scripture, theme, or topic, you might want to review these sermons for resources, illustrations, or helpful insights.

After I've completed the process to this point, I'm ready to start writing the first draft of the sermon. I start with an outline of the sermon. I look for the best way to begin the sermon, the structure of the sermon, and how I hope to end the sermon. I begin thinking of the call to action that I want to include, and then I'll lay out the two or three key ideas I hope to cover. I'm a bit of a perfectionist, so I will typically write or rewrite four drafts of the sermon before I'm finally pleased with it. As noted earlier, by that time I've pretty much got the sermon memorized. I blow it up to 16-point text and print it while sending a copy to our video team so they can see where I've placed any video clips, maps, graphics, and scriptures that will appear on the video screens as I preach. Then I pray once more.

I have the good fortune of preaching five times per weekend. The first of these is Saturday night. At the Saturday night service two or three people have copies of my manuscript and I ask them to take notes while I'm preaching, noting the time throughout the manuscript, and where they feel I could cut, change, or expand various parts of the sermon. This critique is invaluable to me. After Saturday night I have a chance to make a few changes to the sermon based upon this feedback, allowing me to improve the sermon for the four remaining Sunday services. One piece of advice—if you are married, don't ask your spouse to be one of the critics. You will hear criticism of the sermon better from those you're not married to.

Now, having read the process I go through to prepare a sermon, and thinking about your own process for sermon preparation, I invite you to look over the previous chapters once more. Consider how all of the steps fit together, and think about which of the tips and tactics might be most helpful for you.

I'll end with these words, which the Apostle Paul quotes, drawing from the prophets Joel and Isaiah:

> *All who call on the Lord's name will be saved.* So how can they call on someone they don't have faith in? And how can they have faith in someone they haven't heard of?

And how can they hear without a preacher? And how can they preach unless they are sent? As it is written, *How beautiful are the feet of those who announce the good news.* (Rom 10:13-15)

This is our task, fellow preachers, as we seek to speak on behalf of God, proclaiming God's word to the people God has entrusted to our care. It is, in my view, the most important form of public speech.

May your feet be beautiful as you proclaim the good news!

ACKNOWLEDGMENTS

This book would not have been possible without the editorial help and encouragement of Constance Stella, my editor for *Speaking Well*. I'm also grateful for Darrell Holtz, who does a magnificent job developing curriculum at the Church of the Resurrection where I serve. Both of these two helped shape this book as we began having preliminary conversations about what a small book on speaking and preaching might look like. I'm also grateful for Jeffery Moore, who prepared the illustrations for the book. As is the case with all of my books, this book would not have been possible without the love, encouragement, and insights of my wife, LaVon. Finally, I would like to acknowledge my preaching professors in college and seminary, who played an important role in shaping my preaching, Dr. Kenneth Mayton, Dr. John Holbert, and Dr. William McElvaney. I am indebted to their investment in me and thousands of others students they taught.